Penguin Books
Fantastic Paper Gliders

Michael Johnson was born in Yorkshire and graduated from York College of Art. He worked in a major London design studio before becoming a freelance in 1960 and has illustrated and designed for publishing and advertising companies throughout Europe. He spent some time in New York working on magazine illustrations for *McCalls*, *Redbook*, *Cosmopolitan*, and *Good Housekeeping* and, from 1973 until 1975, worked in West Germany as a consultant art director and illustrator. He published an illustrated book, *Angela's Rainbow*, in 1983.

Michael Johnson has also designed a variety of things from furniture to racing-car parts and competition model gliders. He has been interested in aerodynamics and gliders since the age of twelve and, as well as travelling, has also enjoyed cycling and racing cars.

Michael Johnson

FANTASTIC
PAPER GLIDERS

Penguin Books

PENGUIN BOOKS

Published by the Penguin Group
27 Wrights Lane, London W8 5TZ, England
Viking Penguin, a division of Penguin Books USA Inc.
375 Hudson Street, New York, New York 10014, USA
Penguin Books Australia Ltd, Ringwood, Victoria, Australia
Penguin Books Canada Ltd, 2801 John Street, Markham, Ontario, Canada L3R 1B4
Penguin Books (NZ) Ltd, 182–190 Wairau Road, Auckland 10, New Zealand

Penguin Books Ltd, Registered Offices: Harmondsworth, Middlesex, England

First published 1987
10 9 8 7 6 5 4

Copyright © Michael Johnson, 1987
All rights reserved

Filmset in Linotron Imprint by
Rowland Phototypesetting Ltd
Bury St Edmunds, Suffolk

Made and printed in Singapore by Imago Publishing

Sensible protective clothing and safe methods of procedure are essential when knives
and glue are in use. The author and publishers strongly advocate that all safety
instructions recommended by manufacturers be followed rigorously, and they can accept
no responsibility for any ill-effects resulting from the use of adhesives.

CONTENTS

INTRODUCTION

The date of the first model glider is unknown, but for centuries, since people started to understand the basic principles of flight, they have inevitably used models of different kinds in their attempts to design flying machines. The gliders in this book are more sophisticated than the folded-paper darts that excited most of us when we were children, but they perform much better, and the variety of their shapes and sizes is more pleasing.

Building flying machines is a fascinating pastime. With a little patience, anyone over twelve years old will find the gliders in this book relatively easy to assemble, though it would be advisable to tackle one or two of the simpler models first—Blue Max, Stella or White Knight—before launching into the far more demanding Triple Blind, for example. Whether they are simple or more complicated, however, all the gliders are made up of very similar elements, which means that the experience that you acquire in assembling your first example will help you when you move on to other models.

Before you start work, make sure that you have the following equipment at hand.

- A pair of sharp scissors or a sharp little craft knife like a scalpel.
- A ruler, preferably made of metal, since it will be thinner. A plastic or wooden ruler will do, but its edges must be clean and straight.
- Two pieces of wooden dowel, one ⅛" (3 mm) and the other 3/16" (5 mm) in diameter. Both should be at least 11" (280 mm) long. (Dowel can be bought from almost any model or craft-supply store. Alternatively, you may be lucky enough to have access to knitting needles of the required dimensions!)
- Paper glue. It is important to use a glue that is not too liquid, since that will tend to distort the paper. Some glues (balsa cement, for example) shrink on drying, which also leads to distortion unless they are used sparingly. What I have found best for the purpose is stick glue—Pritt Stick is a well-known example. It is very easy and clean to use and is quite strong enough to hold these gliders together.
- A clean, flat surface, such as a plastic-topped table, on which to press out and assemble the parts. Make sure to give yourself plenty of room.

Separate, detailed diagrams and instructions are provided to help you assemble each glider, but you will find the following general instructions useful for all models. Read them first, as they will take much of the risk and sweat out of assembling even the most complicated paper gliders.

GEI ERAL INST UCTIONS

WINGS (see Fig. 1)

- Press out both wings carefully and, using scissors or a knife, cut off any ragged little ends of paper that may have been left behind by the perforations.
- Next, if stiffeners are to be used, turn the wings upside-down on a flat surface and glue the stiffeners on.
- With the wings still upside-down, use your ruler to hold them down along the score lines where a bend is required, and run the back of your knife blade or the point of your scissors across the paper. This will cause the paper to bend up along the scored line. It is best to start with the lines that make up the box-spar section that forms the leading edge of each wing (but don't stick the box section down yet). Take care to do this as neatly and as carefully as possible.

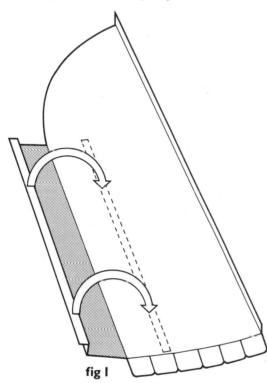

fig I

- When all the scored lines have been given their folds, you are ready to form the curved top of the wing. There are two ways of doing this. Experience will show you which way you prefer.

Rolling

Place the wing on a flat surface, underside uppermost. With one hand place the larger of the two dowels lengthwise in the middle of the wing; with your other hand take hold of the trailing (rear) edge of the wing. Pull the wing gently under the dowel, rolling it as far as the leading edge. Repeat this movement until the wing is curved as required. Make sure that the first (frontmost) third of the wing is slightly more curved than the rest.

fig Ia

WING SECTION

Scoring

Take the ruler and, with the underside of the wing uppermost, very gently score lines about ⅛" (3 mm) apart along the length of the wing, using the back edge of the knife or scissors and working from the leading edge back to the trailing edge. Be careful not to press too hard, or you may go through the paper. This scoring will automatically produce a good, constant curve.

- The next step is to glue into position the box-spar that will form the leading edge under the wings of most gliders. (This is not the case for Triple Blind, for which the paper is simply folded over and glued flat.) With the wings still upside-down, fold and glue the spar section in place, finally using the ruler's edge to press it down firmly. Turn the wing over and gently twist each tip in a slight "washout". This term, which recurs throughout the book, means twisting the trailing edge slightly up at the tip compared with the mid-point of the wing (see fig. 1c). Washout gives the glider greater stability. A glider will fly without it, but it is an important self-regulating device that delays the stall. Take great care that each wing has exactly the same twist.

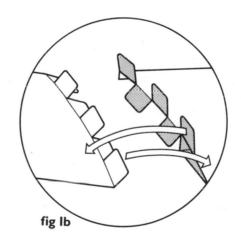

fig Ib

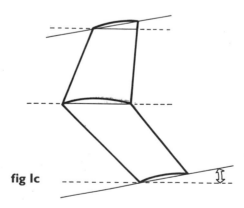

fig Ic

- Check that the wings have been assembled as neatly as possible, with a smooth curve to the top surface. Any wrinkles or uneven twists will make it harder for your glider to perform to the limits of its capabilities.

STABILIZER (see Fig. 2)

The assembly of the stabilizer follows the same principles as that of the wings, only in this case there is no washout of the tips. Not all models, of course, have stabilizers—Delta, Elta and Wings, for example.

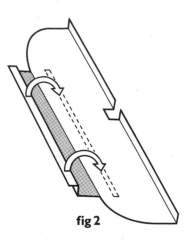

fig 2

fig 2a **STABILIZER SECTION**

FUSELAGE (see Fig. 3)

● Press the fuselage out, and trim away any rough edges. Place it flat on your working surface, the right way up. Lay your ruler along the first scored line (the one by the edge with rounded corners), and bend up this first section by running your knife or scissors under the edge.

● Turn the paper over and roll it carefully around the larger dowel to form a tube. Remove the dowel, and glue the entire length of the first tab with two coats of glue.

● Insert the dowel again, and roll the paper around it until this tab is in position. Press it down firmly with the ruler.

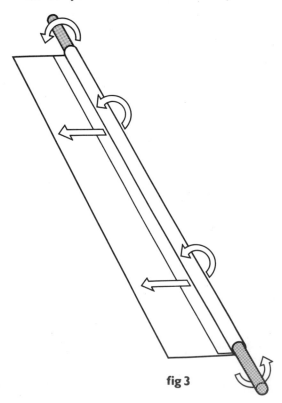

fig 3

● To finish the tube, apply glue to the rest of the fuselage and roll it tightly backwards and forwards, under both hands, on a clean, flat surface. Make sure that the tube has no kinks or bends.

● Slide out the dowel (you may find that it comes out more easily if you twist it a little), and remove any glue that may have stuck to it. When you are satisfied that the dowel is completely clean, insert it in the tube once again and set the fuselage aside to dry.

TAIL FIN (see Fig. 4)

The last element to be prepared is the fin.

● Fold the paper carefully to form the section shown in fig. 4a.

● Glue only at the edges. If, after gluing, you find that the fin has flattened out too far, you can restore the correct section by sliding a scissor point inside.

● Make sure that there are no uneven twists. Set the fin aside to dry.

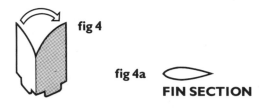

fig 4

fig 4a **FIN SECTION**

ASSEMBLY

Now that the separate parts of the glider are completed, assembly can begin.

● The wings should be dry by now. Check that they are perfect mirror images of each other—identical in section and in washout, and in every other way.

● On each wing you will see a row of tabs. These must be bent alternately upwards and downwards (see fig. 1b). Any tab that encroaches on the spar section when bent down should be cut off.

● Place the wings together in a trial fitting to make sure that the tabs interlace correctly, as fig. 1b shows. When you are satisfied with the fit, take each wing in turn and apply two coats of glue to each tab. If you are in any doubt about which side of each tab to glue, refer to fig. 1b.

● Fit the wings accurately together, and press the tabs firmly in place, starting in the middle and working out to each edge. You will notice that on all the gliders the junction between the wings is slightly curved: the purpose of this is to give you automatically the correct section and attitude for each wing—as long as you take care over the assembly.

● Now, before the glue dries completely, is the time to hold up the wings and view them carefully—from the rear is best—to check that they are well lined up, with identical washout. If they are not, you should still have time to make adjustments by gently bending and pulling before the central joint is quite dry.

● Glue the wing joiner in place under the leading edge, and set aside to dry completely.

● The remainder of the assembly is chiefly a matter of attaching the parts to the fuselage. For this purpose, leave the dowel inside the fuselage tube, as it will prevent you from flattening the tube as you press on the different parts.

● Place the fuselage on the table and glue on first the wing mounts, then the stabilizer mounts, taking care that their lower edges follow the line of the fuselage exactly. The detailed assembly instructions for each model will make clear the correct placing in every case, as well as giving guidance on the attachment of stiffeners in models that use them.

- Next, take the wings and glue them into position on the tabs of the wing mounts. Be careful to keep the wings quite square to the fuselage, since a small variation will cause the glider to turn to one side or the other. Then fit the stabilizer in the same way, making absolutely sure (by viewing from behind) that it lines up accurately with the wings and is not tilted.
- The fin should be positioned on the fuselage exactly as shown in the small colour photograph of each model that you will see on the model pages. It is easily attached by the two glued tabs.
- Make one final check that everything is square—the glue will dry all too quickly! Now at last you can remove the dowel from the fuselage.
- Most of the models require an extra weight (a small roll of paper) in the nose. You will need to coil this quite tightly: either roll it around itself or, if you prefer, use a toothpick or cocktail stick to help you. Insert the weight in the nose of the fuselage tube, and you will find that it uncoils like a spring to fit snugly inside.
- You are almost ready to fly your glider—but not quite! Before doing so you must check that the point of balance is in the right place. (The place varies from model to model: check the detailed assembly instructions.) If the glider is nose-heavy, pull out the nose weight, carefully cut a small piece off the end and insert it again until the glider balances. A few gliders may be tail-heavy: the solution here is to add a little more paper to the nose weight. When the balance is correct, glue the weight in position. (These remarks do not apply to certain of the gliders, which are so designed as to need no extra weight, as their point of balance falls naturally in the right position. These are Sky Shark, Chroma Canard, Wings, Delta and Elta.)
- With some models—White Knight, Canary, Blue Max, Triple Blind, Gyro, and Green Sweep—a slightly better glide may be achieved if their weight is reduced by leaving off the stiffeners for the wings and wing mounts. This should be done with discretion, however, as the omission of the stiffeners will affect the gliders' durability.

TRIMMING AND FLYING

The glider is now ready for the first trimming flights.

These are best done indoors—a room with a clear length of 16 feet (5 metres) is just big enough, but something larger is preferable. Out of doors you will need a flat-calm day with no wind at all. And if it's recently been raining, you'll have to postpone the event: damp can have disastrous effects on the paper that you have carefully assembled.

Before making the first flight, check, by looking down the fuselage with one eye (from the rear), that there are no warps in the wings or stabilizer. It's worth making a habit of this brief check before every flight. As you'll discover when you start to fly your planes, the tiniest deformity in the shape can have far-reaching effects on the flight. Make any necessary corrections by gentle bending. The final check is to examine the extreme trailing edge of the wings and stabilizer. These should be turned down at an angle of 90° for the wings and 45° for the stabilizer.

At last, the moment of truth: your very first flight.

Balance the glider on your hand, and hold it at the point where it balances, then gently launch it with wings level and nose pointing slightly downwards. Your movement should be as smooth as possible. Don't throw the glider with a jerky motion, and never point the nose upwards.

The ideal glide should be as long and as floating as possible, with no tendency to stall or dive. (Fig. 5 shows flight angles and the terms used to describe them.) If the glider shows signs of either of these, adjustment to the trailing edge of the stabilizer should put things right. If the model tends to dive, for example, reduce the angle of the trailing edge from 45° to perhaps 10°—in other words, reduce the amount by which it is bent down. If it stalls—if its nose rears up and then drops—bend down the trailing edge a fraction more.

Remember, any adjustment you make should be very small. The size of these gliders is such that the difference between a stall and a dive can be as little as 1/16″ (1.5 mm). Experiment cautiously, and you will soon get a feel for the kind of adjustments that are necessary.

If, after these various small adjustments, you are still not getting a good glide, or if the glider has an erratic flight pattern, check all flying surfaces for warps. You may find that something is out of line. For example, the wings may have unequal twist, or the stabilizer may be bent. Rectify this by gently bending the offending part into the correct shape.

All these gliders are designed to be flown in quite restricted areas, but they can be flown from high windows or hillsides, provided that they are trimmed properly and the weather is very calm. For this sort of flying it is best to trim a glider so that it flies in large circles (to prevent it from flying too far away!). This can be done by bending the trailing edge of the fin left or right, as desired. You will find that the tighter the turning circle, the less the trailing edge of the stabilizer will need to be turned down. Adjust this edge until you have the perfect flat glide.

One final word of warning: if you trim your glider to fly in circles, and then manage to get it drawn into a thermal (warm air rising, sometimes to thousands of feet), that may well be the last you see of it. It will climb higher and higher in slow, lazy circles until directly overhead it disappears out of sight— or OOS, as glider flyers say.

Good luck!

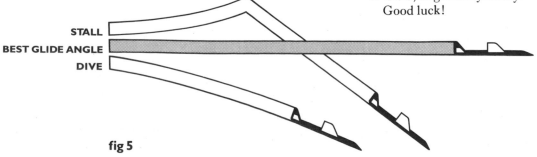

STALL
BEST GLIDE ANGLE
DIVE

fig 5

CANARY

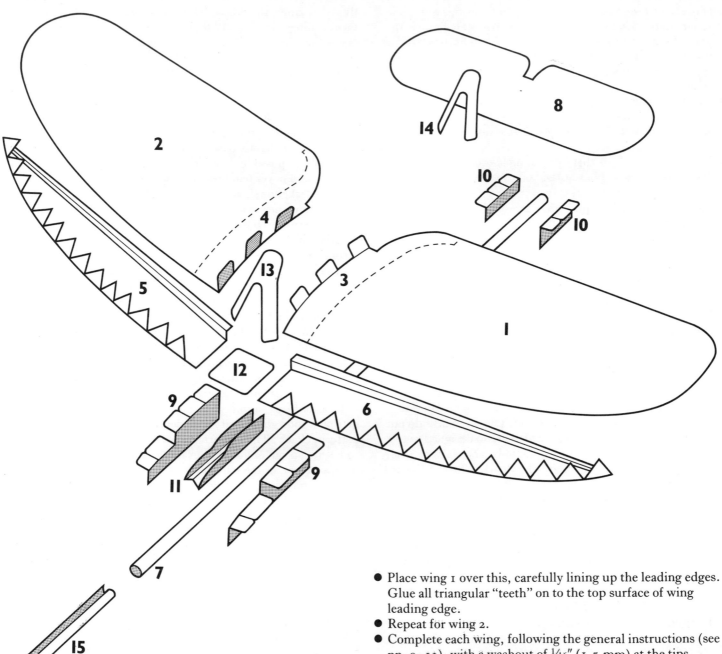

This is the smallest glider in the book. It has a good glide, partly because of the sawtooth edge to the wing. This turbulates the airflow over the top surface, improving the glider's flying qualities.

The construction follows the general instructions (see pp. 9–11), apart from the wings, which are built as follows.

- Press out the wings (1 and 2), wing stiffeners (3 and 4), wing spars (5 and 6) and wing joiner (12).
- Glue the stiffeners (3 and 4) to the underside of each wing, taking care to align them with wing-joint line.
- Bend the spar section (6) to the shape shown in the drawing, with sawtooth edges bent up.

- Place wing 1 over this, carefully lining up the leading edges. Glue all triangular "teeth" on to the top surface of wing leading edge.
- Repeat for wing 2.
- Complete each wing, following the general instructions (see pp. 9–11), with a washout of $1/16''$ (1.5 mm) at the tips.
- Make up the stabilizer (8).
- Roll the fuselage tube (7) around a $1/8''$ (3 mm) dowel or knitting needle. Glue securely. When the fuselage is dry, attach the wing mounts (9), stiffener (11) and stabilizer mounts (10) in the positions marked.
- Go back to the wings. Glue them carefully together, ensuring that the washout is the same for each, then glue the joiner (12) under the central joint of the box section.
- When all is dry, glue the wings in place, followed by the strap (13); next, glue the stabilizer and strap (14).
- To balance the glider, roll up the weight (15) and insert it in the nose of the fuselage tube. Adjust until the glider's point of balance is $1/2''$ (13 mm) in from the trailing edge of the wings. When you are satisfied, glue the weight into position.
- Trim and fly according to the general instructions (see pp. 9–11).

SKY SHARK

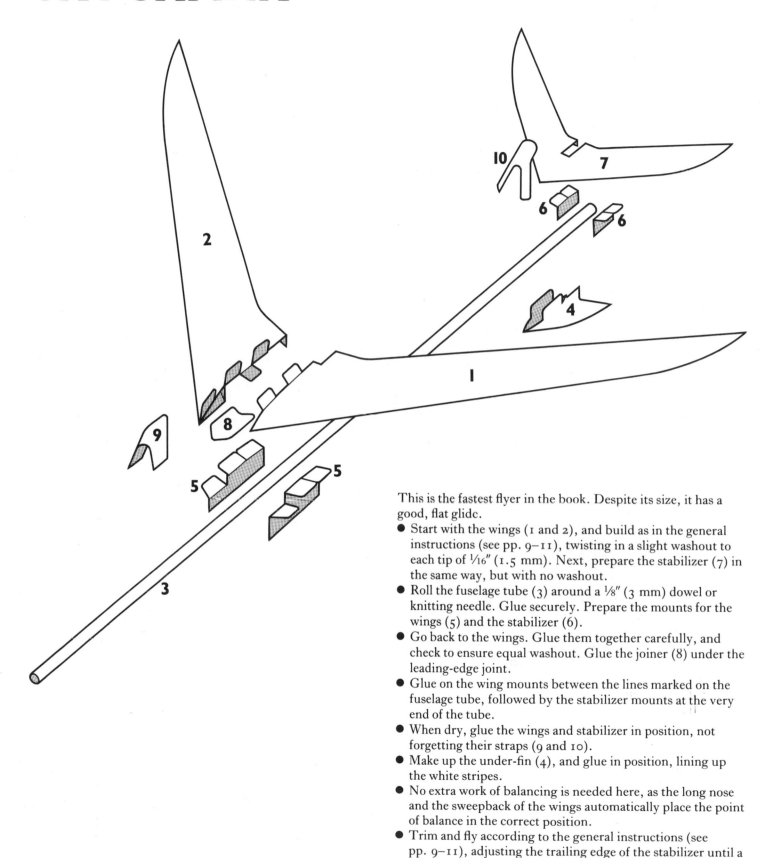

This is the fastest flyer in the book. Despite its size, it has a good, flat glide.

- Start with the wings (1 and 2), and build as in the general instructions (see pp. 9–11), twisting in a slight washout to each tip of 1/16″ (1.5 mm). Next, prepare the stabilizer (7) in the same way, but with no washout.
- Roll the fuselage tube (3) around a 1/8″ (3 mm) dowel or knitting needle. Glue securely. Prepare the mounts for the wings (5) and the stabilizer (6).
- Go back to the wings. Glue them together carefully, and check to ensure equal washout. Glue the joiner (8) under the leading-edge joint.
- Glue on the wing mounts between the lines marked on the fuselage tube, followed by the stabilizer mounts at the very end of the tube.
- When dry, glue the wings and stabilizer in position, not forgetting their straps (9 and 10).
- Make up the under-fin (4), and glue in position, lining up the white stripes.
- No extra work of balancing is needed here, as the long nose and the sweepback of the wings automatically place the point of balance in the correct position.
- Trim and fly according to the general instructions (see pp. 9–11), adjusting the trailing edge of the stabilizer until a long, flat glide is obtained. Alternatively, as I found with one of the prototypes, the best glide may be achieved by adjusting the trailing edge of the wing, so that it has a 90° turndown in the middle and about 10° at the tips. Experiments will show which is better in your case.

BLUE MAX

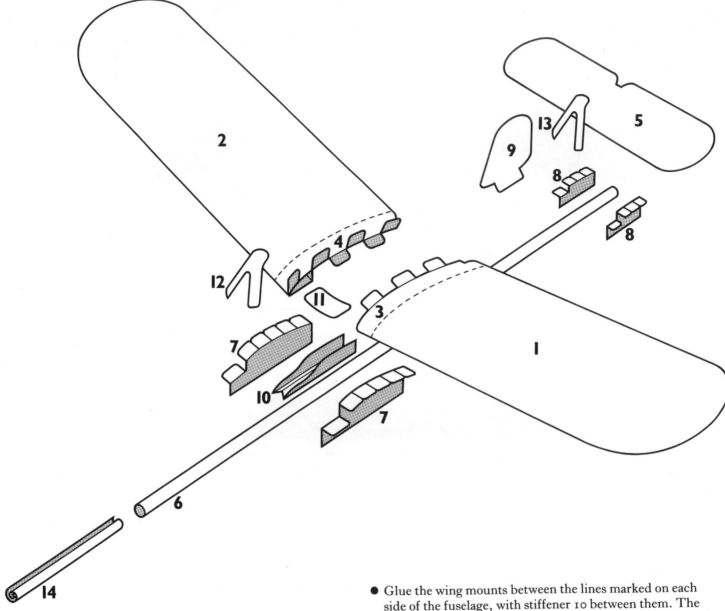

Simple to assemble and attractive when completed, this is the ideal model to make first. It also has a good, easily trimmed glide.

- Starting with the wings (1 and 2), glue on the stiffeners (3 and 4) and complete, following the general instructions (see pp. 9–11). Twist in a ⅛″ (3 mm) washout at the tips.
- Make up the stabilizer (5) in the same way, but no washout is needed.
- Roll the fuselage (6) around a ³⁄₁₆″ (5 mm) dowel or knitting needle. Glue securely. Prepare the mounts for the wings (7), the tail (8) and the wing-mount stiffener (10).
- Glue the wings together carefully, checking from the rear to ensure that the washout is the same on both, then glue the joiner (11) under the central joint of the two wing spars.

- Glue the wing mounts between the lines marked on each side of the fuselage, with stiffener 10 between them. The stabilizer mounts should then be glued in line with the end of the fuselage tube.
- Glue the wings in position on the tabs provided on the mounts, ensuring that all is square. Then glue the wing strap (12) over the front part of the wing joint and on each side of the fuselage.
- Fit the stabilizer in a similar way, checking from the rear to ensure that it is in line with the wings. Then glue on the strap (13).
- Fold and glue the edges of the fin (9) together, making sure not to distort its shape by gluing it flat. Then glue it to the fuselage, as shown in the photograph.
- Roll up the nose weight (14), slide it into the nose of the fuselage tube, and adjust so that the glider's point of balance is ⅝″ (16 mm) in from the trailing edge when the model is held under the wings.
- Trim and fly, following the general instructions (see pp. 9–11).

CHROMA CANARD

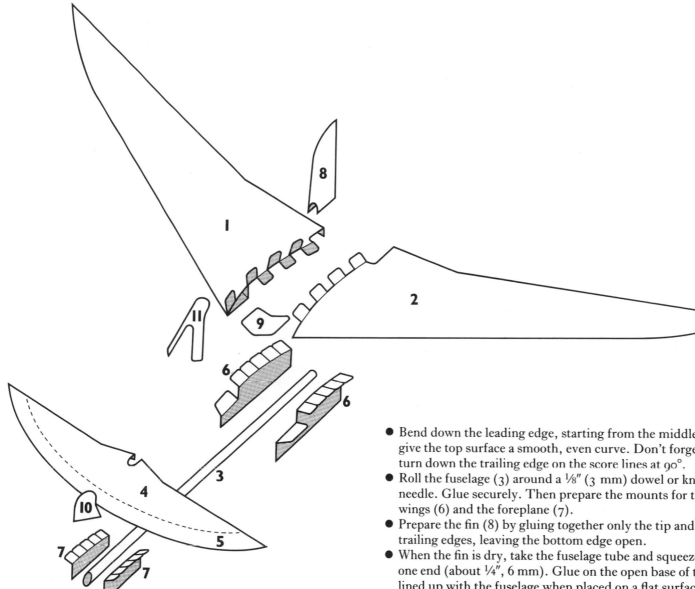

This intriguing glider follows the Canard design, in which the stabilizer is mounted *in front* of the main wing, not behind, as in conventional aircraft. This means that when the aircraft approaches a stall, the foreplane stalls first, while the mainplane remains unstalled. In full-sized aircraft, this is a major safety feature.

This model glider has a very good glide, as you will see. Flying into a stall, it will tend to bob up and down like a porpoise until trimmed correctly.

- Start by making up wings (1 and 2), as in the general instructions (see pp. 9–11). Twist in about ⅛″ (3 mm) washout on each tip.
- Prepare the foreplane (4) by gluing the stiffener (5) in position under the leading edge.

- Bend down the leading edge, starting from the middle, to give the top surface a smooth, even curve. Don't forget to turn down the trailing edge on the score lines at 90°.
- Roll the fuselage (3) around a ⅛″ (3 mm) dowel or knitting needle. Glue securely. Then prepare the mounts for the wings (6) and the foreplane (7).
- Prepare the fin (8) by gluing together only the tip and trailing edges, leaving the bottom edge open.
- When the fin is dry, take the fuselage tube and squeeze flat one end (about ¼″, 6 mm). Glue on the open base of the fin, lined up with the fuselage when placed on a flat surface.
- Glue the wing mounts (6) in position, so that the back tab of each overlaps slightly each side of the fin.
- Proceed to the foreplane mounts, gluing them in line on the other end of the fuselage tube, which should now be cut off at the angle formed by the front edges of the mounts.
- Glue the wings together carefully, checking from the rear to ensure that they are aligned and identical. Glue on the joiner (9) under the leading-edge joint.
- Glue the wings in position with the central "slot" on each side of the fin. Next glue on the wing/fuselage strap (11).
- Glue the foreplane on to the front mounts and, finally, glue the nose strap (10) over the foreplane and point of the fuselage.
- The Chroma Canard is now ready to trim and fly.
- Trimming, in this case, is done by small adjustments to the *foreplane*—that is, if it stalls, take *up* a fraction of the trailing edge. If by chance it dives, reverse the effect by turning *down* the trailing edge.
- I find that bending down the *leading* edge of the foreplane cures any "porpoising" tendencies.

RAINBOW MAGRITTE

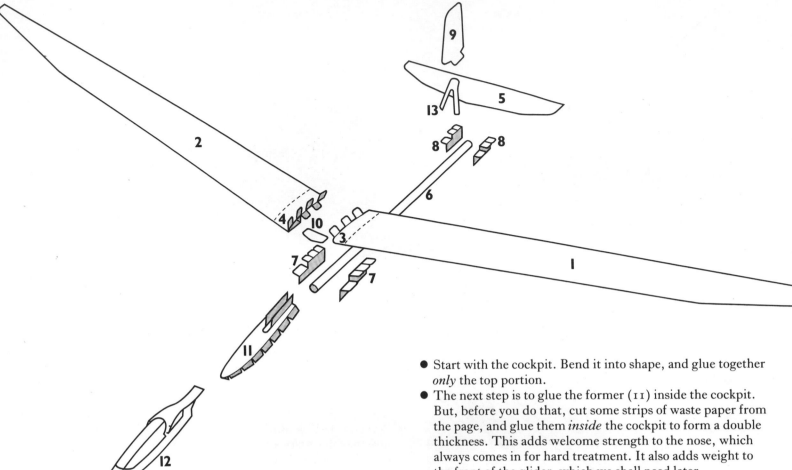

● Start with the cockpit. Bend it into shape, and glue together *only* the top portion.

● The next step is to glue the former (11) inside the cockpit. But, before you do that, cut some strips of waste paper from the page, and glue them *inside* the cockpit to form a double thickness. This adds welcome strength to the nose, which always comes in for hard treatment. It also adds weight to the front of the glider, which we shall need later.

● Now glue the former from the nose to halfway under the wing.

● Position this half-finished section on the wings/fuselage with the long tab behind the cockpit over the central section of the wings, and the tabs of the former on each side of the wing mounts, under the wings. If this fits perfectly, glue it in position, with the nose pointing slightly down in relation to the line of the fuselage tube. If, by chance, it does not fit perfectly, before gluing in position use scissors to trim the end of the fuselage tube at an angle, and any edges or corners of the former (11).

● For the next step it is necessary to turn the glider upside-down, resting it on a small pile of paperback books to avoid damaging the wings.

● Having placed the glider in position, glue together the underside of the cockpit, leaving two tabs unglued at the extreme nose. (You will need to slide in more weight later.)

● Finish fitting the stabilizer (5), stabilizer strap (13), and fin (9).

● You now need to get the point of balance in the correct place. Do this by rolling up pieces of scrap paper and sliding them into the nose until the glider balances ¼" (6 mm) from the trailing edge, underneath the wing.

● Trim for flying as in the general instructions (see pp. 9–11). You will find that, when built and trimmed correctly, this glider has a beautiful, flat glide rather like that of a full-size sailplane in miniature.

● Start by preparing the wings (1 and 2). Glue on the stiffeners (3 and 4), and continue to build up the wings according to the general instructions (see pp. 9–11). In this model, the washout on the wings, about ⅛" (3 mm), starts only on the last third towards the tip. The remaining two-thirds of the wing should have no twist at all.

● The wings are long and narrow, and require a little more care than usual in construction. Try to be as precise as possible, for any small error will be magnified along the length of the wing.

● Make up the stabilizer (5) in the same way.

● Roll the fuselage tube (6) around a ³⁄₁₆" (5 mm) dowel or knitting needle. Set aside to dry, and go back to the wings.

● Glue the wings together carefully. Ensure that the washout of the two wings is equal, and fit the joiner (10).

● Fit the wing mounts (7) between the lines marked on one end of the fuselage tube. Follow this with the stabilizer mounts (8) on the opposite end.

● Glue the wings carefully in position.

● Now press out and prepare the nose and cockpit (12) and the internal former (11).

STELLA

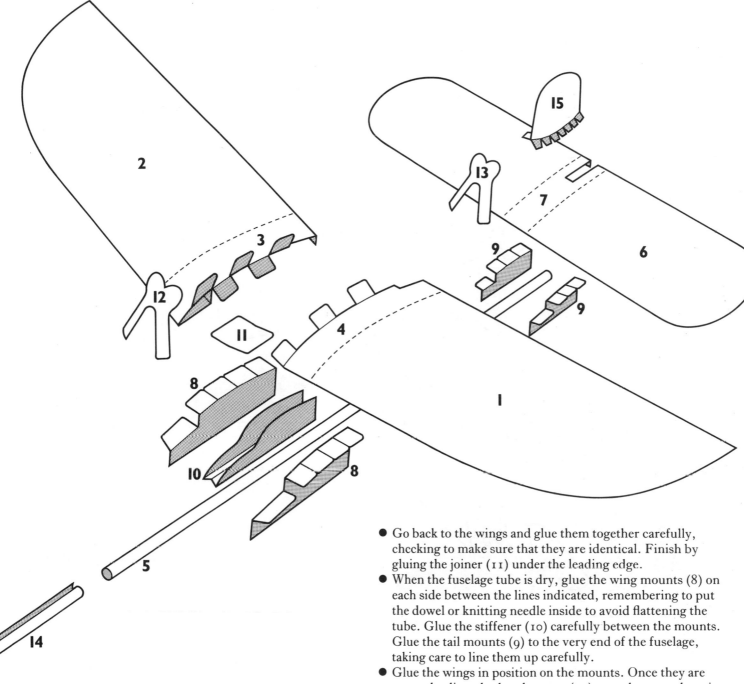

This glider, with its ample proportions, is one of the simplest to build.

- Start with the wings (1 and 2), glue on the stiffeners (3 and 4), and continue to build up by following the general instructions (see pp. 9–11). In this case, the washout on the wing tips should be ¼" (6 mm). When both are complete, set aside to dry.
- Make up the stabilizer (6), not forgetting to glue on the central stiffener (7) first.
- Roll the fuselage (5) around a ³⁄₁₆" (5 mm) dowel or knitting needle, then glue securely. Again, follow the general instructions.

- Go back to the wings and glue them together carefully, checking to make sure that they are identical. Finish by gluing the joiner (11) under the leading edge.
- When the fuselage tube is dry, glue the wing mounts (8) on each side between the lines indicated, remembering to put the dowel or knitting needle inside to avoid flattening the tube. Glue the stiffener (10) carefully between the mounts. Glue the tail mounts (9) to the very end of the fuselage, taking care to line them up carefully.
- Glue the wings in position on the mounts. Once they are correctly aligned, glue the strap (12) over the central section and around each side of the fuselage.
- Glue the stabilizer into position and, after checking the alignment from the rear, add the strap (13).
- Make up the fin (15) by folding and gluing together. Take care not to glue it flat.
- When the fin is dry, glue it in position on the stabilizer, up to the slot.
- When all is dry, roll up the weight (14), and fit it inside the nose, adding or subtracting weight until the glider's point of balance is ¾" (2 cm) in from the trailing edge of the wings.
- Trim and fly following the general instructions (see pp. 9–11). You will find Stella has a beautiful, slow, floating glide when trimmed correctly.

THUNDER BIRD

The design of this glider was conceived as a miniature eagle, and if care is taken over its construction and trimming, you will be rewarded with truly bird-like flying qualities.

- Start by building up the wings (1 and 2), as in the general instructions (see pp. 9–11). Give the wing tips a washout of ³⁄₁₆″ (5 mm).
- Build up the stabilizer (4). There should be no washout.
- Roll the fuselage tube (3) around a ³⁄₁₆″ (5 mm) dowel or knitting needle. Glue securely.
- Glue the wings together carefully, checking from the rear to ensure that the washout is the same on both. Glue the wing joiner (11) in position.
- The fuselage should now be dry. Glue the wing mounts (5) in position between the lines marked on the fuselage tube. Glue on the stabilizer mounts (6), lined up with the other end of the tube. Carefully glue the wings in position on the wing mounts, checking to make sure that they are at right angles to the fuselage.
- To create the "body" of the bird, glue formers 7 and 8 inside section 9, as shown. Carefully bend to shape, and glue the "head" section (10) together. Set aside to dry.
- Glue the body section (9) into position on each side of the wing mounts and under the wings. This is best done if the whole fuselage/wings assembly is turned upside-down and placed on a small pile of paperback books or small box to protect the wings.
- Fit and glue the head section in position, with the top tab overlapping the middle section of the wing, the feather-shaped tabs around the body, and the round hole of the front flush with the end of the fuselage tube. (*Don't* glue the "beak" on yet.)
- Once all this is neatly glued together, fit part 12 by gluing the feather-shaped tabs over the top of the middle of the wing joint, and the two side tabs around each side of the head and under each wing.
- Glue the stabilizer in position, followed by the strap (13).
- Now you'll see why the "beak" has not yet been glued on. First you need to roll up the weight (made from scrap paper) in the front of the fuselage tube, flush with the front of the "head". Do this, and adjust until the bird's point of balance is about two-thirds of the way back from the leading edge of the wing.
- Once this is done, glue the weight in position, and finish by gluing on the "beak" (14).
- One suggestion: before fitting the "beak", glue scraps of paper inside it, as these strengthen it considerably and will prevent it from being damaged in flight.
- Trim in the usual way by bending the stabilizer down or up as required.
- I find that the best glide is obtained by bending down slightly the leading edges of the last quarter of the wings at the tips. If you try this, make sure that the curve is smooth and constant.

TRIPLE BLIND

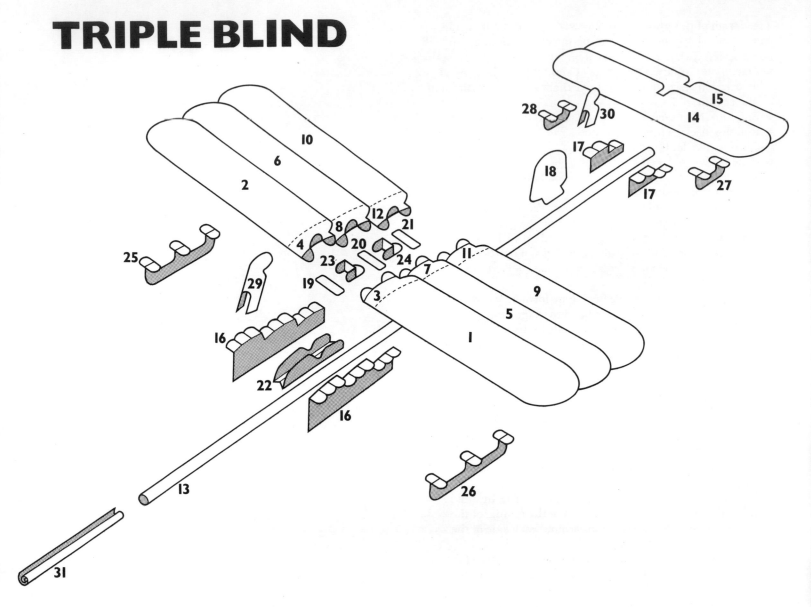

This is a very attractive model when completed, but there is no doubt that it is the most complicated in the book to make. It has more parts to glue together than any other model, and, because of its three wings and two stabilizers, it needs more care, not only in building but also in trimming and flying. Having said this, if the assembly is not rushed, and if care is taken with the wings and stabilizers, it should pose no problems. It will just take more of your time than the others!

● Carefully press out the wings and their stiffeners. Glue stiffener 3 under wing 1, stiffener 4 under wing 2, stiffener 7 under wing 5, and so on, until all six wing halves are ready for the next operation.

● You will notice that this model has no box-section spar. The strength of the leading edge is achieved simply by folding and gluing a triple thickness of paper.

● Place each wing upside-down on a flat surface, and roll with a dowel or knitting needle until a gentle, smooth curve is obtained.

● When you have all six wing halves ready, take wing 1 and fold along the score lines so as to form the strengtheners under the leading edge. Do this by placing the wing upside-down, folding back the first part of the scored section and gluing it flat. Then glue the second part back over on the first to form the third thickness of paper. Press completely flat with your ruler. Repeat this for all the wings. When they are dry, place them upside-down again, and *gently* make three or four scores, close together, along the whole length of the leading edge. You will find that this gives the required curve.

- Repeat the same method for the two stabilizers (14) and (15).
- Make up the fuselage tube (13) as in the general instructions (see pp. 9–11), using a ⅛″ (3 mm) dowel or knitting needle.
- Fit the wing mounts (16) between the two lines marked, and fit the stiffener (22).
- Complete the fuselage assembly by gluing the stabilizer mounts (17) on to the very end of the tube.
- Go back to the wings and glue them all together, 1 to 2, 5 to 6, and 9 to 10. Check from the rear to ensure that they all match, with no twist at all (yet!) and with the same angle. Don't forget the wing joiners (19, 20 and 21) under each leading edge.
- Glue wings 9 and 10 firmly in position on the rear and lower "step" of the wing mounts, making sure that they are perfectly square.
- Glue strap 24 over the middle of the wing and over each side of the wing mount.
- Glue the second pair of wings, 5 and 6, on the middle "step" of the wing mount, followed by strap 23.
- The last pair of wings is glued on the top and foremost "step" of the wing mount. When they are properly aligned, glue on strap 29.
- Prepare the wing "struts" (25 and 26) by folding and gluing together, as shown in the diagram.
- Fit the wing "struts" in position under each set of wings, about halfway between wing tips and fuselage. Take care not to position them incorrectly: when held up, they should be in line with the slope of the three wings.
- Use the same method to fit the two stabilizers (14 and 15), their "struts" (27 and 28) and the stabilizer strap (30). Then fit the fin (18), placed ¾″ (2 cm) from the leading edge of the stabilizers.
- Glue in the nose weight (31), adjusting it so that the glider's point of balance is under the middle of the rear wing.
- Before trimming, give a slight washout to each wing by bending down *slightly* the leading edge of each tip for about the first 1″ (2.5 cm). Remember to make them all identical!
- Check the glider from the rear, and make sure that the slots between wings and stabilizers are exactly the same on each side. Ensure, too, that there is no uneven warp when one side is compared with the other. It is important for the glide quality that wings and stabilizers be checked very carefully; otherwise the glider will follow all sorts of erratic and unwanted flight patterns.
- To trim, adjust the trailing edge of the rearmost stabilizer.
- A final suggestion: I find it useful to make small adjustments to the tip washout (by bending down the leading edges) until the best glide is obtained.

DRAGONFLYER

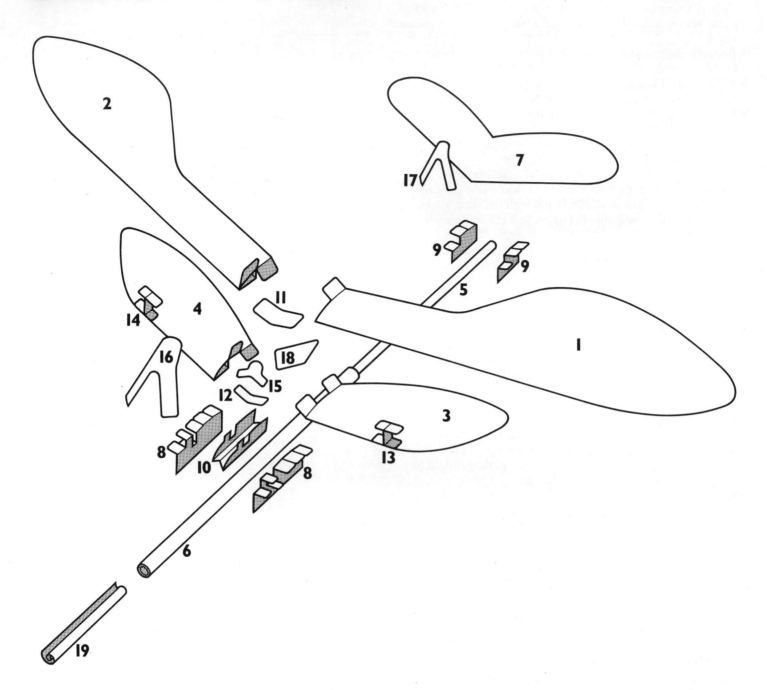

This glider is based on the wing forms of various insects, although its wings are fixed. It has a slight "biplane" look, the top wings forming a "slot" over the lower smaller wings to give it an almost stall-free glide.

If it is put together and trimmed correctly, you will find that, when faced with a situation in which other gliders would stall, it just "wallows" slightly, then carries on gliding.

- Start with the wings. Take wings 1 and 2 and build them up, following the general instructions (see pp. 9–11). Follow with wings 3 and 4, and then the stabilizer (7).
- The fuselage is in two parts. Make up part 5 by rolling it around a $^3/_{16}$" (5 mm) dowel or knitting needle. Roll part 6 around one end of part 5 to form a fuselage tube whose front half is thicker (and stronger) than the other. This has the advantage of giving a little extra weight at the front end.
- When all is dry, glue into position the wing mounts (8) and the stiffener (10) between them, with the front edge of the mounts on the dividing line between the orange and the purple.
- Glue the stabilizer mounts (9) on the other end.
- Glue wings 1 and 2 together, twisting in a very slight washout of their tip portions. Glue together the smaller wings (3 and 4), this time with no washout.
- Make sure that the upper and lower wings are at the same angle to the fuselage, and have the same sweep-back, by placing one over the other and comparing them. Adjust them, if necessary, before the glue is completely dry. When you are satisfied, fit the joiners (11 and 12).
- Make up the two small wing "struts" (13 and 14) by folding and gluing them together, leaving tabs at the top and bottom.
- Glue the lower wings in position on the rear half of the wing mounts. When they are aligned, fit strap 15 over the central leading edge and over each side of the wing mounts.
- Fit the small wing "struts" in position, as shown in the diagram.
- Glue the top wings in position, ensuring that the overlap of the lower wings is the same on both sides. Join the upper and lower wings together by means of the wing "struts" that are already glued to the lower wing, checking underneath to make sure that everything is aligned.
- Glue strap 16 over the central section of the top wings, down each side of the wing mounts and around the fuselage tube.
- Fit the stabilizer according to the instructions on pp. 9–11. Glue on the stabilizer strap (17).
- To complete the assembly of the glider, glue the wedge-shaped piece (18) in the middle of the lower wings, with the point overlapping and aligned with the fuselage.
- Roll up the weight (19), insert it in the nose, and adjust so that the glider's point of balance falls $^1/_8$" (3 mm) behind the back edge of the wing mount.
- Before trimming, check from the rear that all gaps between the upper and lower wings are equal and that the upper wing tips have retained their slight washout.
- The red lower wings should have their trailing edges curving slightly downwards.
- Trim by adjusting the rear edge of the stabilizer and, if necessary, by bending down very slightly the leading edge of the top wing tips.

GYRO

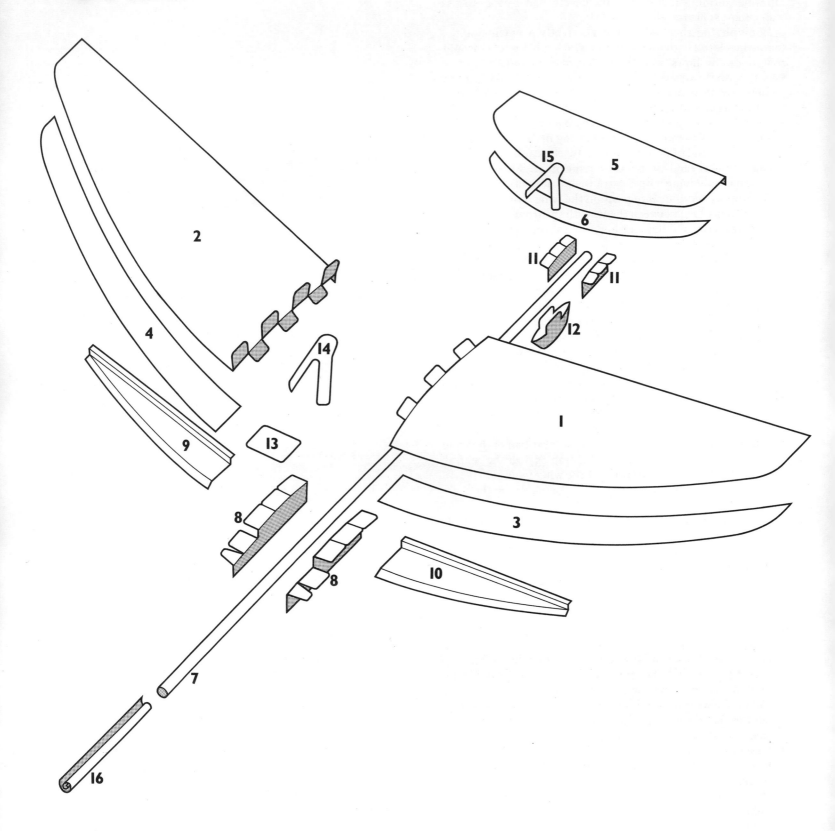

This simple little glider has good flying characteristics, and can be trimmed to fly in quite tight circles, if you wish. As you can see from the drawing, the spar section is fitted separately under the wings, not just folded under as in the case of most of the other models.

● Starting with the wings (1 and 2), glue on the stiffeners (3 and 4) inside the leading edge under each wing. (This is best done with the wings upside-down.) Then line up the curve of the stiffeners with the curve of the leading edge. When they are glued in position, press them down flat with a ruler.

● Work in the curved section of the wing, either by rolling or by gently scoring underneath (see general instructions, pp. 9–11).

● Fold the spar sections (9 and 10) to shape, as shown in the diagram, and glue them under each wing in turn, lining them up with the middle of the wing and slightly overlapping the inside curve of the stiffeners. Twist in a slight washout of 1/16" (1.5 mm).

● When they are dry, bend down the leading edge of each wing to give a little more curve to the wing section, and then bend down the trailing edge at a 90° angle, using the ruler to make a good, clean edge.

● The stabilizer (5) is made in the same way.

● Roll the fuselage tube (7) according to the general instructions (see pp. 9–11), using a 1/8" (3 mm) dowel or knitting needle.

● Go back to the wings. Glue them carefully together, checking to ensure that there is no uneven warp, and that the washout on each tip is identical. When you are satisfied, glue the wing joiner (13) under the leading edge.

● Glue the wing mounts (8) on each side of the fuselage, with their back edges in line with the end of the black nose section.

● Glue the wings in position. When they are all square, glue on the strap (14).

● Glue the stabilizer mounts (11) on either side of the fuselage. Glue the stabilizer in position, and fit the strap (15). If you wish the glider to turn *left* and fly in circles, glue the stabilizer mounts on to the fuselage at such an angle that the stabilizer is positioned with a slight tilt to the *right*—that is, so that the stabilizer is aligned with the *left* wing when viewed from the rear.

● Fold and glue the fin (12) in position under the fuselage up to the stabilizer strap.

● Roll up and insert the weight (16) in the nose of the fuselage. Adjust the weight until the glider's point of balance is 1/2" (13 mm) from the trailing edges under the wings.

● Trim by adjusting the trailing edge of the stabilizer.

● A gliding turn will be built in if you have glued the stabilizer on at a tilt. If you would prefer a larger turning circle, glue the stabilizer on straight, and bend the trailing edge of the fin slightly. You will find that the tighter the turn, the less turn-down you will need on the trailing edge of the stabilizer.

WINGS

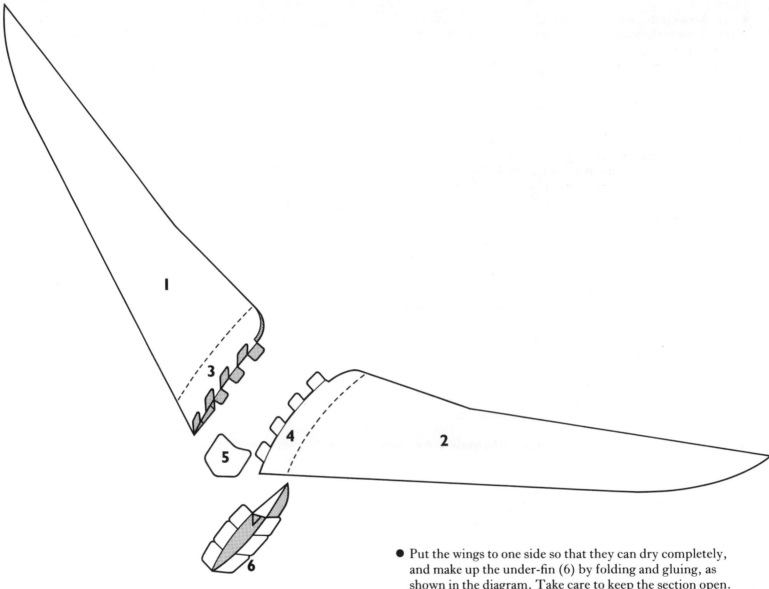

As you see, this is an all-wing, or tail-less, glider. If care is taken with the washout at the wing tips, it has a very good glide. One of the reasons for this is the glider's lack of weight; also, its point of balance falls in the correct position because of the careful distribution of the very few parts.

- Prepare both wings (1 and 2). Glue on the stiffeners (3 and 4), and proceed to make up the wings according to the general instructions (see pp. 9–11). In this case, I suggest that you score each wing to form the curved section, but score only the first third back from the leading edge. At the tip of each wing, bend down the leading edge slightly along the curve. When the spar section has been glued, but is not yet quite dry, twist in 1/16" (1.5 mm) of washout at the tips. Check the washout carefully by placing the wing flat and measuring under the trailing edge in line with the end of the spar section.

- Put the wings to one side so that they can dry completely, and make up the under-fin (6) by folding and gluing, as shown in the diagram. Take care to keep the section open.
- Go back to the wings and glue them together, taking great care to ensure that the washout at the tips is equal. When you are satisfied, glue on the joiner (5).
- Glue the under-fin, with the "point" up, to the spar section, and glue the fin (red) between the joint of the two rounded trailing edges.
- Trimming must be done carefully, so check again, from the rear, to make sure that the washout at the tips of the wings is equal.
- Now check the turned-down lip of the trailing edge of both wings. The angle of the lip should be 90° at the mid-point of the wing and about 30° at the tip. Try a few flights, and correct by adjusting the lip *at the tip only*. Cure a stall by bending the lip down a fraction; cure a dive by bending it up a fraction. Remember that the same adjustment must be made to both lips.
- Keep adjusting until a long, flat glide is obtained, with no undulations. The best glide is sometimes achieved by flattening the end of the spar section underneath, towards the tips.

DELTA

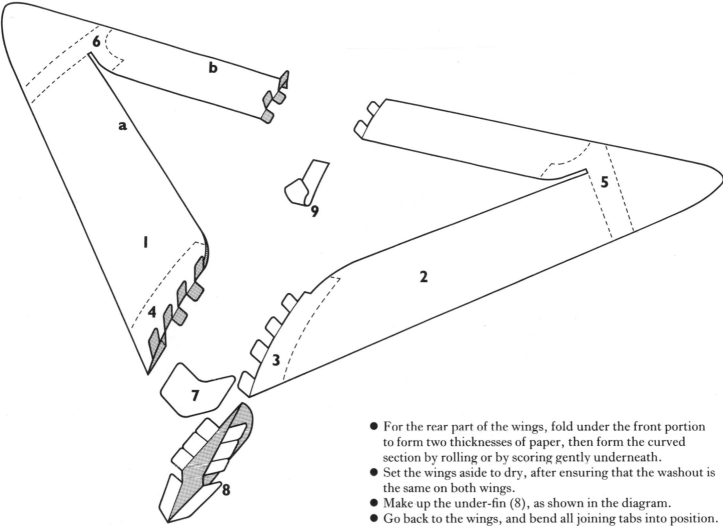

This model, with its excellent glide, was developed only after numerous prototypes and many hours of study. As you can see, it is an *open* delta—that is, it consists of a triangular delta wing with the middle cut out—which leaves the leading and trailing edges (with their own wing sections) to form the flying surfaces. The design has successfully overcome certain problems that a normal delta shape experiences at low flying speeds. The cutaway inside "corners" also help to improve the glider's stall characteristics.

- Start with the wings (1 and 2). Glue on stiffeners 3 and 4 under the wing joints, and stiffeners 5 and 6 under the corner of each tip.
- Make up the wings, following the general instructions (see pp. 9–11). Form the box-section spar under the leading edges, and twist in a washout of ³⁄₁₆″ (5 mm) near the wing tips.

- For the rear part of the wings, fold under the front portion to form two thicknesses of paper, then form the curved section by rolling or by scoring gently underneath.
- Set the wings aside to dry, after ensuring that the washout is the same on both wings.
- Make up the under-fin (8), as shown in the diagram.
- Go back to the wings, and bend all joining tabs into position. After making sure that everything will fit together, start by gluing the "pointed" end together. When this is secure, join the back, trailing edges very carefully: the angle and fit of this joint are very important.
- After checking from the rear that both sides have equal washout, glue on the joiners (7 and 9).
- Glue on the under-fin.
- To trim, first ensure that the tips of the trailing edges on the front "V" (see the point marked A) are at 90° and that the rearmost edge (B) is at about 45° at the middle and about 10° at the very tips. Before flying, bend down slightly the front edge of the rear part of the wing to form a gentle curve, and the leading edges of the front V shape, from the "nose" to the tips.
- Adjust the glide, correcting stall or dive by making small adjustments (downwards or upwards) of the lip at the trailing edge.
- I find that the best glide is obtained with the trailing-edge lip turned down at an angle of about 40° in the middle and about 5° at the tips. Don't touch the turned-down lip of the front V-shaped portion. This should be at an angle of 90° all the way from the curved mid-point around the under-fin into the other two inside corners, which are important, as they enhance the glider's stability.

ELTA

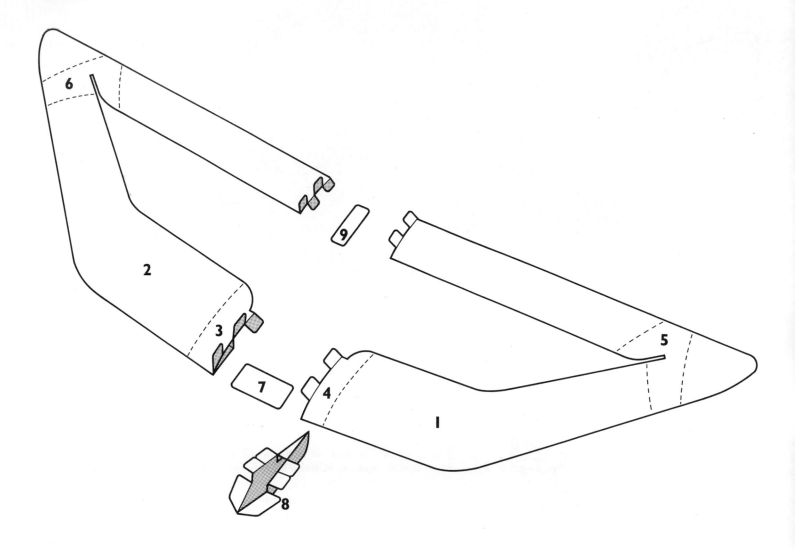

Elta is a development of Delta, but its nose section is flat rather than pointed. As you can see, the assembly of the glider is almost identical to that for Delta except for the critical building of the forward part.

- Start by pressing out the two wing halves (1 and 2). Then glue on stiffeners 4 and 5 under wing 1, and stiffeners 3 and 6 under wing 2.
- Roll a shallow curve on all surfaces, front, swept-back part and rear, paying special attention to the leading edges.
- Fold the spar section, and glue it under the front part first, taking care that the wing is completely flat. Then glue the spar section under the swept-back portion towards the tips, twisting in a slight washout of $1/16''$ (1.5 mm).
- Fold under the front edge of the rear section to form two thicknesses of paper, then give it a slight curve, by gently rolling or scoring, to form the wing section.
- The completion of Elta is exactly as given in the instructions for Delta, beginning at the paragraph that starts: "Make up the underfin . . ." The only exception is that, in trimming, you should turn down the leading edge on the very front to form a smooth curve up to and around the corners as far as the tips.

GREEN SWEEP

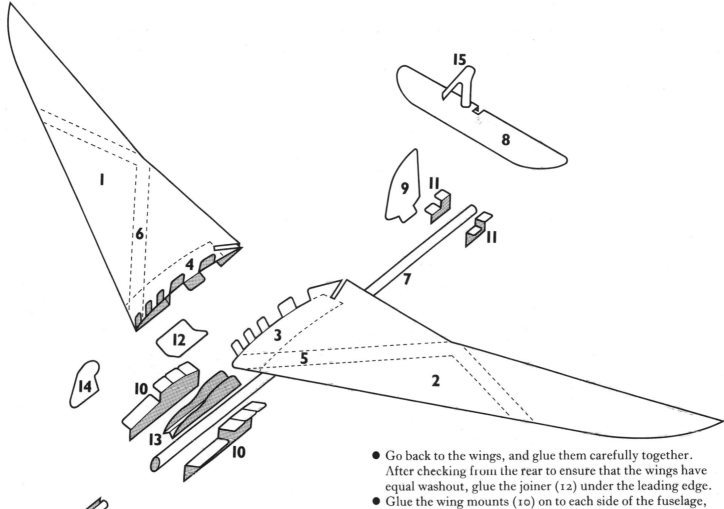

The bird-like shape of this glider is based on the wings of a swift, after studies I made of this bird a few years ago. If care is taken in construction, it has an excellent glide.

- Start by pressing out the wings (1 and 2), plus the stiffeners (3, 4, 5 and 6).
- Place the wings upside-down and glue on stiffeners 5 and 6 in the position seen in the diagram. Now glue on stiffeners 3 and 4.
- Make up each wing in turn according to the general instructions (see pp. 9–11), with washout at the tips of ¹⁄₁₆″ (1.5 mm) measured 2″ (50.8 mm) in from each tip.
- Make up the stabilizer (8) in the same way. (No washout is needed here.)
- Follow this by rolling the fuselage tube (7) around a ¹⁄₈″ (3 mm) dowel or knitting needle.

- Go back to the wings, and glue them carefully together. After checking from the rear to ensure that the wings have equal washout, glue the joiner (12) under the leading edge.
- Glue the wing mounts (10) on to each side of the fuselage, with their front edges in line with one end. Glue the stiffener (13) between them.
- Glue the stabilizer mounts (11) in line with the other end.
- Glue the wings in position on the tabs of the wing mounts, ensuring that the point of the wing joint is central at the front, and that the point formed by the two slots at the trailing edge is exactly in line with the middle of the fuselage.
- Glue on the stabilizer, the stabilizer strap (15) and the fin (9), which should be positioned on top of the fuselage, ³⁄₄″ (19 mm) from the leading edge of the stabilizer.
- Roll up the weight (16), and insert it into the nose of the fuselage. Adjust it so that the point of balance of the glider is ³⁄₈″ (9 mm) in from the trailing edge under the wings, and glue the weight in position.
- Cut off the end of the fuselage at the angle made by the front edges of the wing mounts, and glue the blue "nose" (14) over the front edge of the wing joint and on each side of the fuselage.
- Trim and fly by adjusting the turned-down trailing edge of the stabilizer.
- You may find that the best glide is obtained by adjusting the turned-down trailing edge of two-thirds of the wings at an angle of 90°, and the trailing edge of the tips at an angle of about 5°.

MAVRO

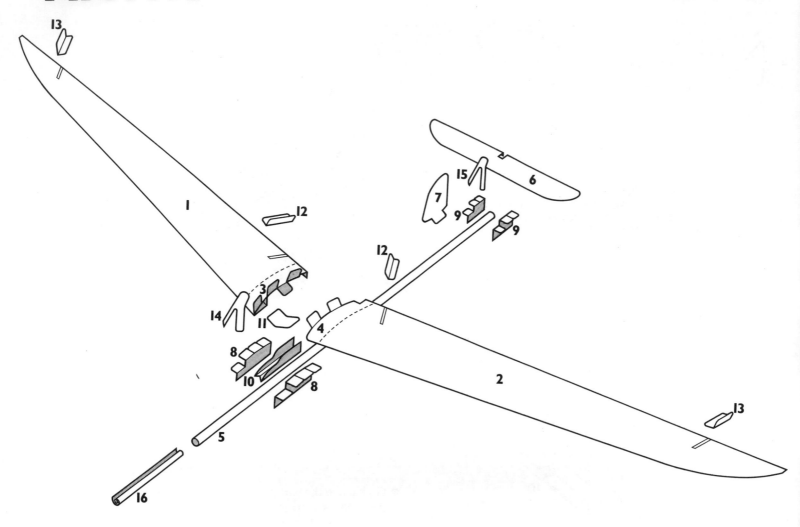

This glider—*mavro* means "black" in Greek—has a good, efficient glide. The small "fences" (12 and 13) in the middle of the wings and at their tips are designed to improve the local airflow over these areas—and, to judge from tests carried out indoors, they certainly appear to improve the stall and glide characteristics of the model.

- To assemble Mavro, follow the general instructions (see pp. 9–11), starting with the wings (1 and 2). Glue on the stiffeners (3 and 4), and build the wings up carefully, as they are long and narrow. Glue the wings together, finishing with the wing joiner (11) under the leading edges. Washout should be ¹⁄₁₆″ (1.5 mm) near the tips, and the "fences" (12 and 13) should be glued on the marks indicated on top of the wings, at an angle of about 45° to the wing surface.
- Make up the stabilizer (6) in the same way.
- Roll the fuselage tube (5) around a ⅛″ (3 mm) dowel or knitting needle.

- Fit the wing mounts (8) between the lines marked on the fuselage tube, with the stiffener (10) between them.
- Glue the stabilizer mounts (9) in position at the other end of the fuselage tube.
- Glue the wings on to the wing mounts, and, after making sure that they fit correctly, glue on the strap (14).
- Glue the stabilizer into position, then glue on its strap (15).
- Fold and glue together the fin (7), taking care to keep its shape, and glue it in position on the fuselage tube.
- Adjust the weight (16) to establish the glider's point of balance on the back edge of the wing mounts, under the wings, and trim following the general instructions (see pp. 9–11).
- I find with this glider, as with some of the others, that the best glide is obtained by adjusting the turned-down trailing edge of the wings at 90° for most of each wing, and at about 5° for the last 2½″ (63 mm) at the tip.

WHITE KNIGHT

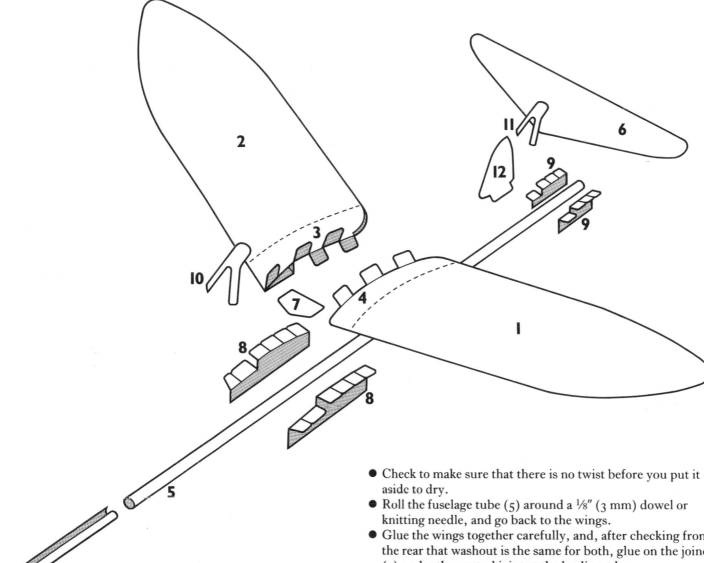

This is one of the easiest gliders to build in the book; its glide is also among the best—always provided that it is carefully put together. If you have never built a glider before, try one of the others first—Blue Max or Stella, for example. Afterwards, when you come back to White Knight, you will find it simple to construct, and you will be able to make it perform at its best. If you feel adventurous, however, don't let me prevent you from going straight on to White Knight!

- Start with the wings (1 and 2). Glue on the stiffeners (3 and 4) and follow the general instructions (see pp. 9–11) to form the box-spar section under each wing. When they are formed, twist in washout of ⅛″ (3 mm) under the trailing edges, 2″ (50 mm) in from the tip.
- When the glue is dry, make sure that the leading edge of each wing is turned down in a smooth curve by pressing the first part of the box spar underneath to form the section shown in the diagram.
- Make up the stabilizer (6) in the same way, folding and gluing each leading edge in turn to form the box section underneath.

- Check to make sure that there is no twist before you put it aside to dry.
- Roll the fuselage tube (5) around a ⅛″ (3 mm) dowel or knitting needle, and go back to the wings.
- Glue the wings together carefully, and, after checking from the rear that washout is the same for both, glue on the joiner (7) under the central joint at the leading edge.
- Glue the wing mounts (8) on to each side of the fuselage tube between the lines marked.
- Next, glue on the stabilizer mounts (9).
- Glue the wings in position with the front "point" and the rear cutaway parts of the wing joint perfectly in line with the fuselage. When this is done, glue on the wing strap (10) so that it overlaps the front of the wings and its ends straddle the fuselage.
- Glue the stabilizer and stabilizer strap (11) in a similar way.
- Fold and glue the fin (12) together, taking care to keep its shape, and glue it in position on the fuselage, as shown in the photograph.
- If you wish, you can glue two thin strips of paper inside the edges of the rounded cutaway trailing edges at the fuselage joint, to give them a slightly better finish.
- Roll and insert the weight (13). Adjust until the point of balance is ⅜″ (9 mm) behind the back edge of the wing mount on the fuselage. (It can be as far back as this because of the sweepback of the wings.)
- Trim, following the general instructions (see pp. 9–11). Adjust the trailing edge of the stabilizer until a long, flat glide is obtained.

ASSEMBLY KITS

SKY SHARK

BLUE MAX

3 4 7 7 8 9 8

1 12 13 6 11 2 10 5 14

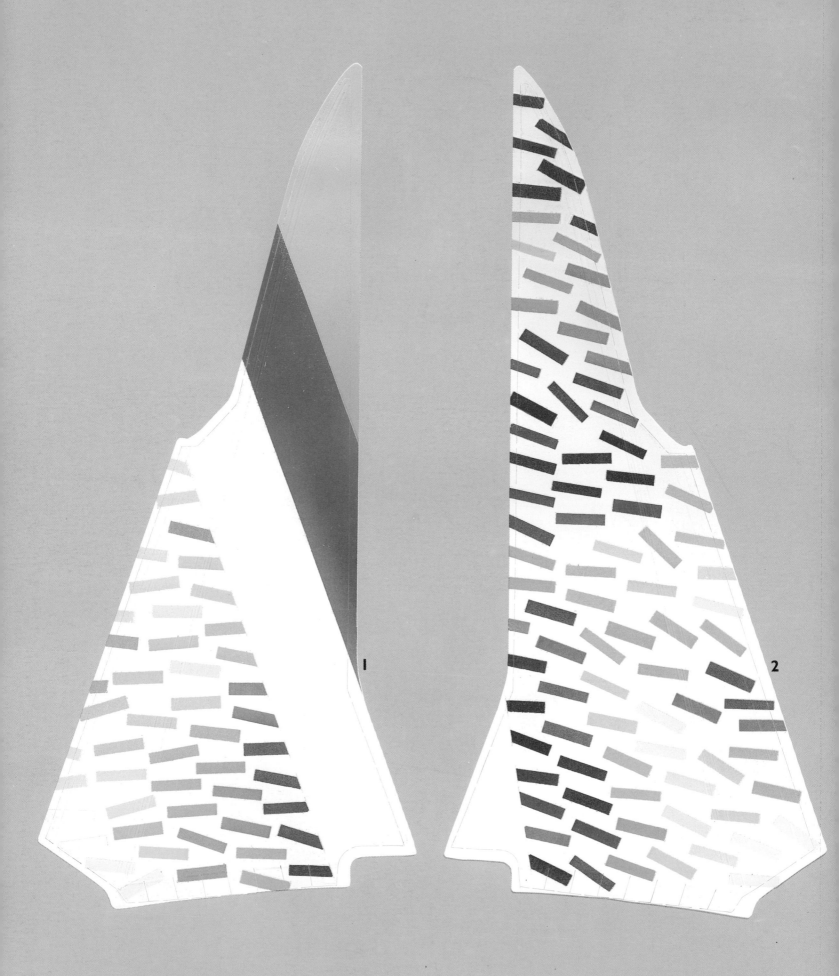

1 2

C ROMA CANA RD

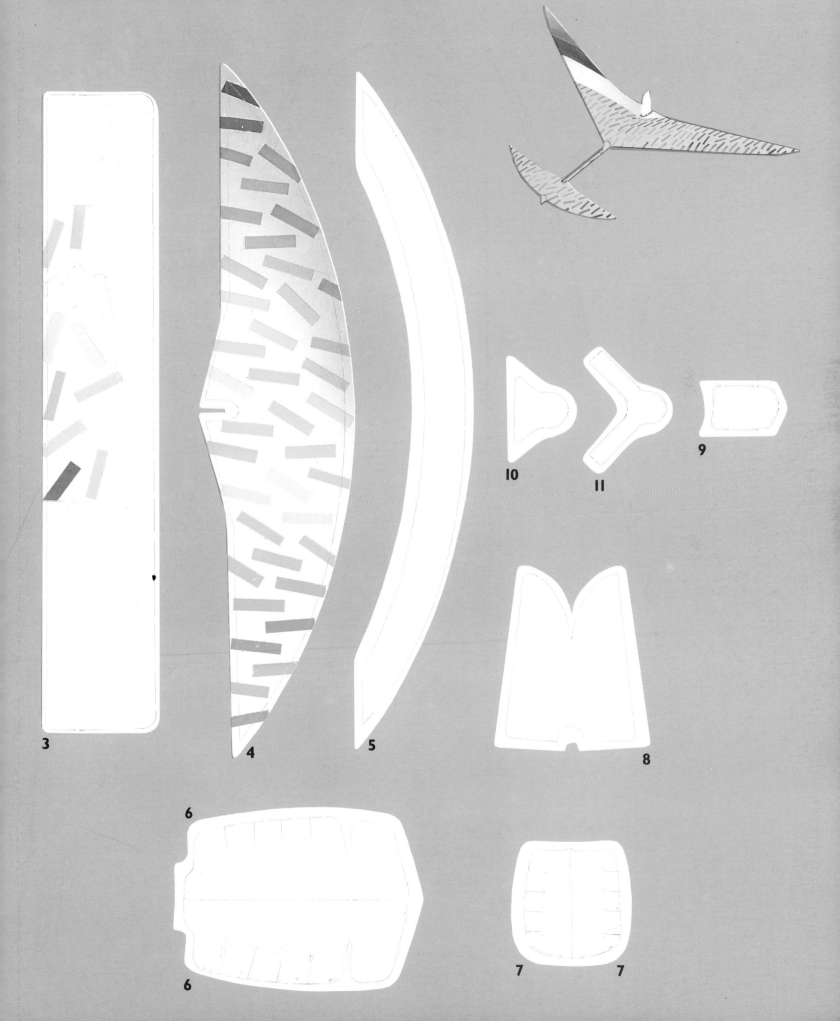

3

4

5

6

6

7   7

8

9

10   11

RAINBOW MAGRITTE

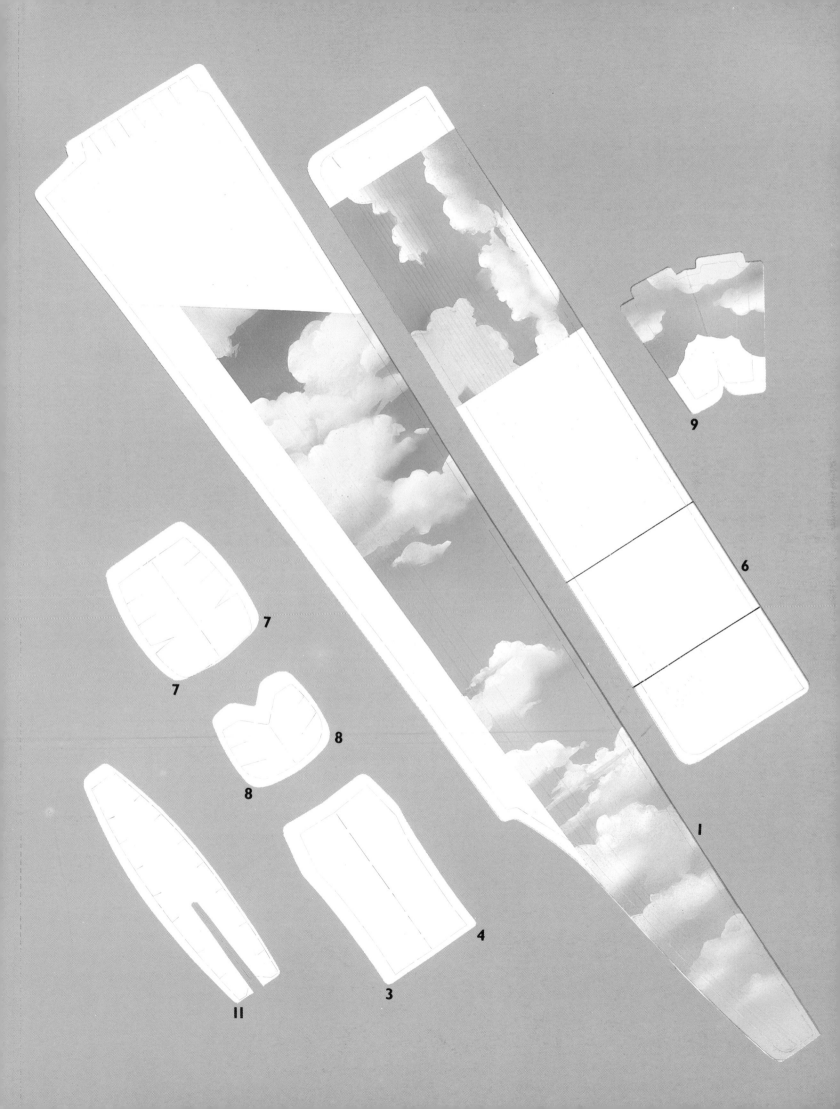

1

10

7

13

12

15

STELLA

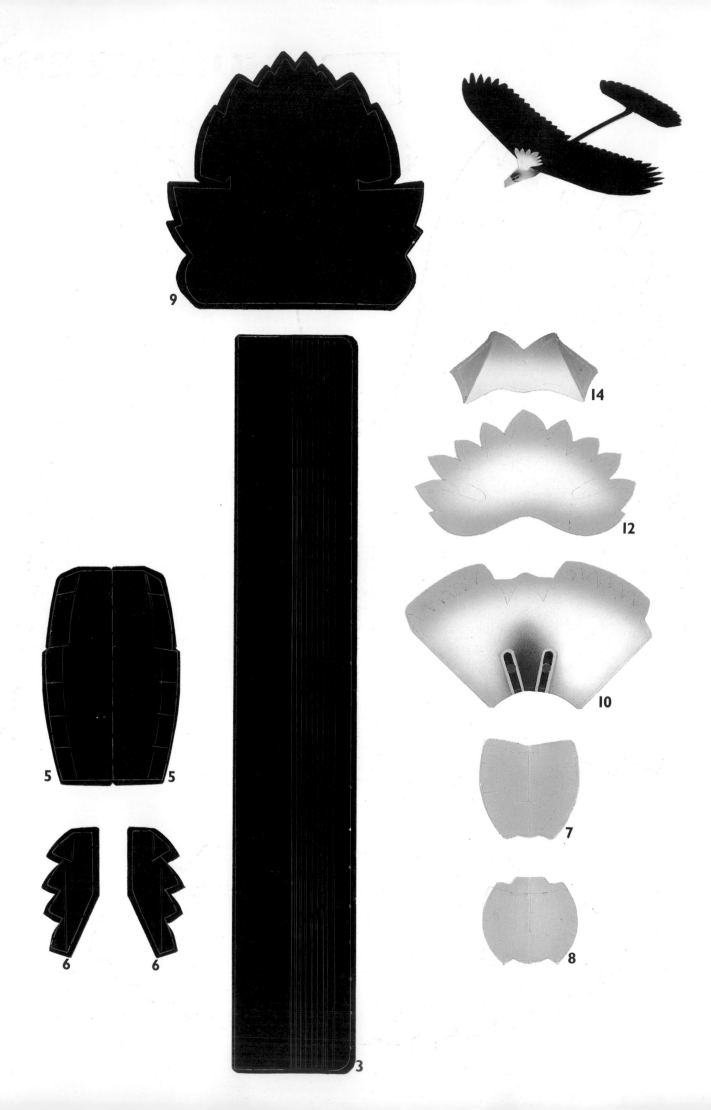

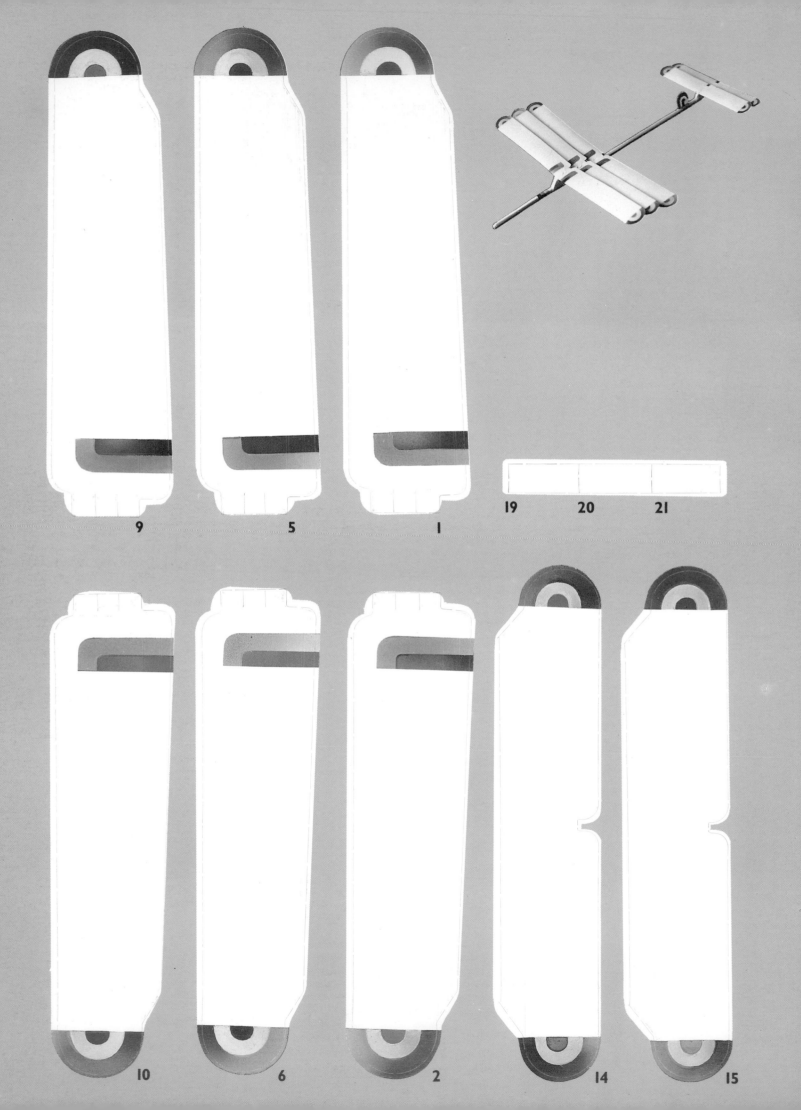

9   5   1   19   20   21

10   6   2   14   15

TRIPLE BLIND

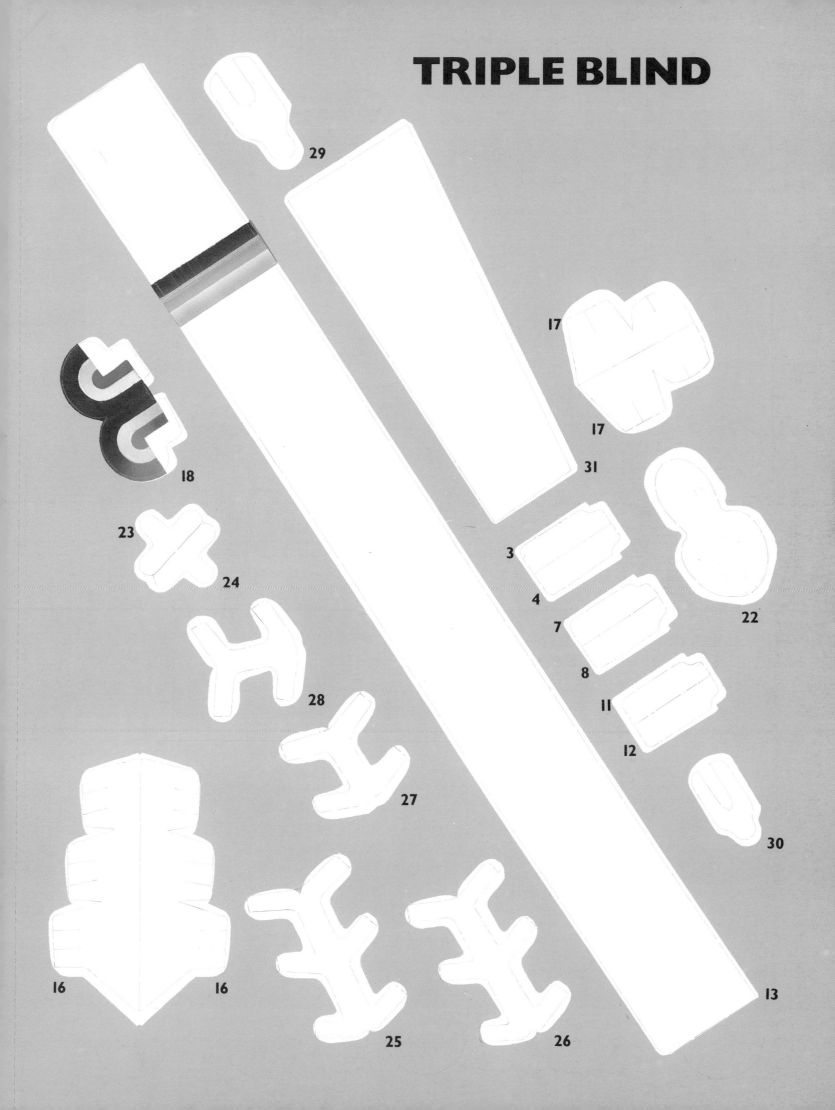

DRAGONFLYER

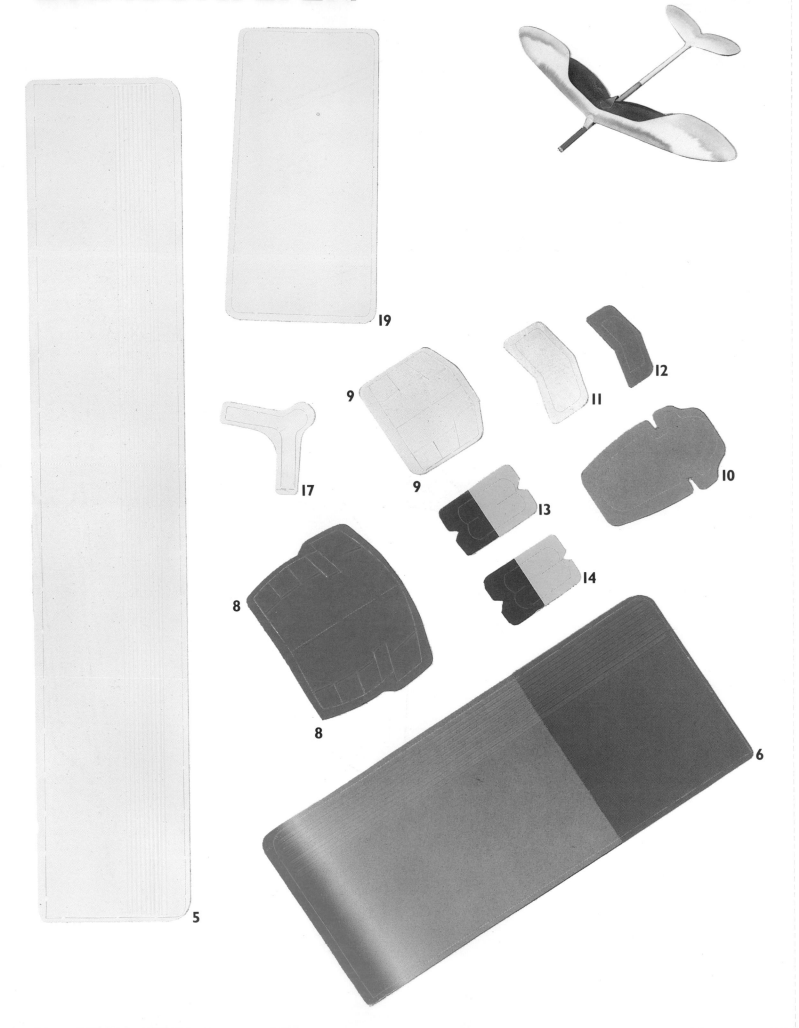

5

19

17

9

9

11

12

13

10

14

8

8

6

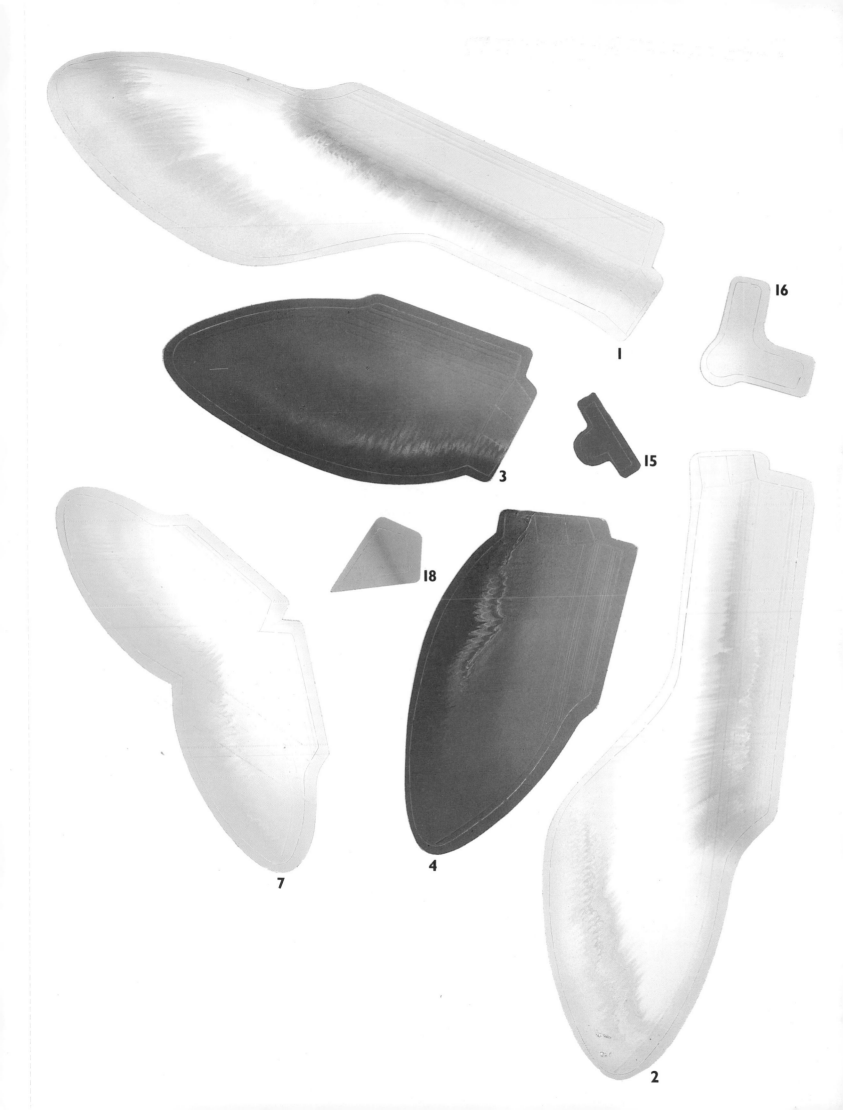

GYRO

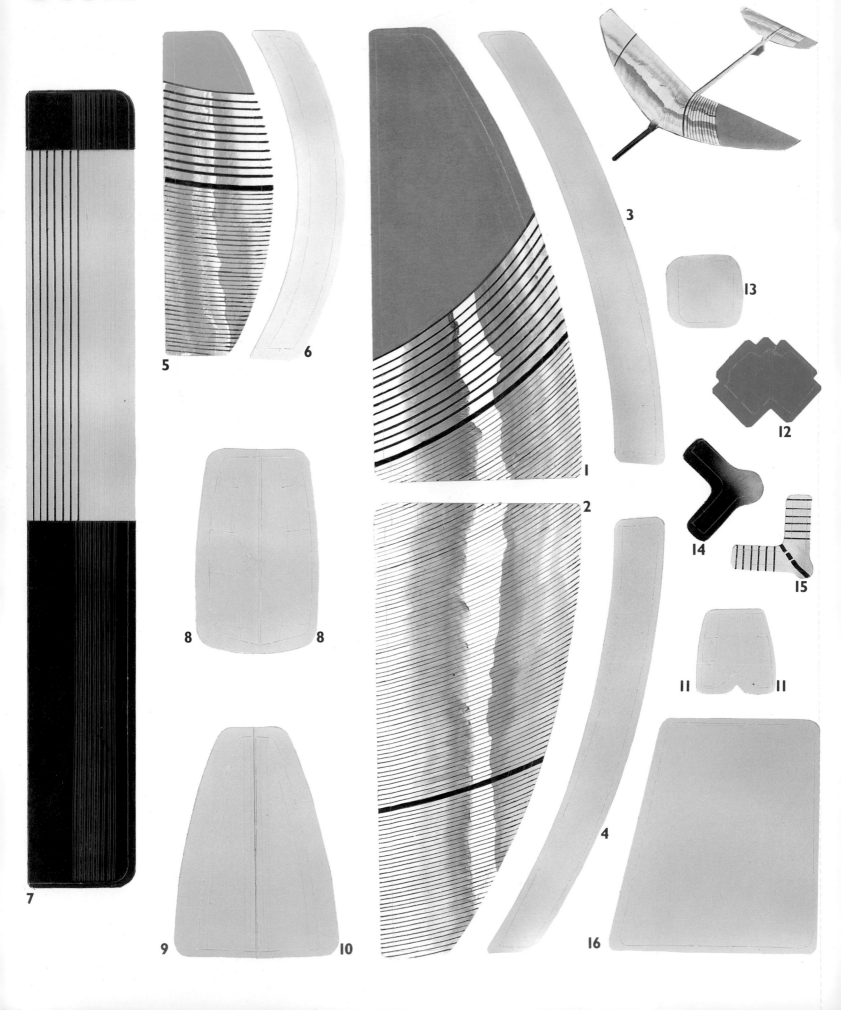

WINGS

1

2

3

4

5

6

DELTA

ELTA

GREEN SWEEP

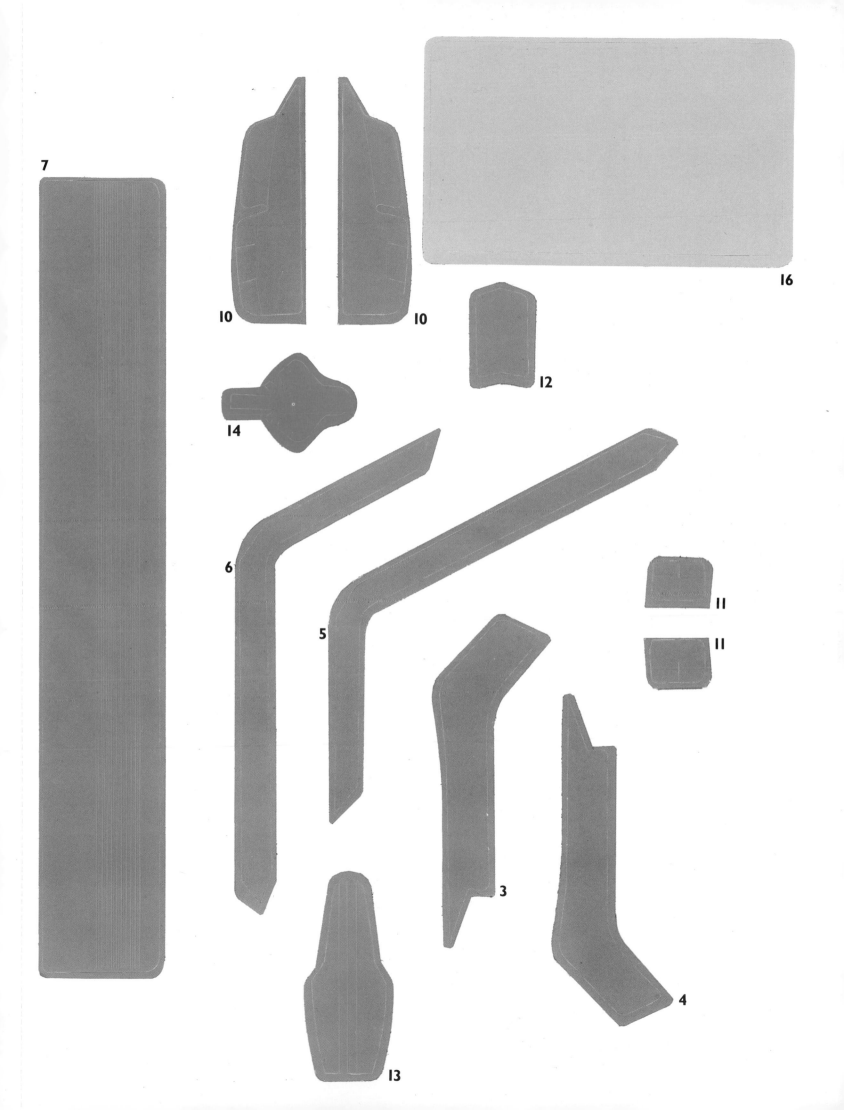

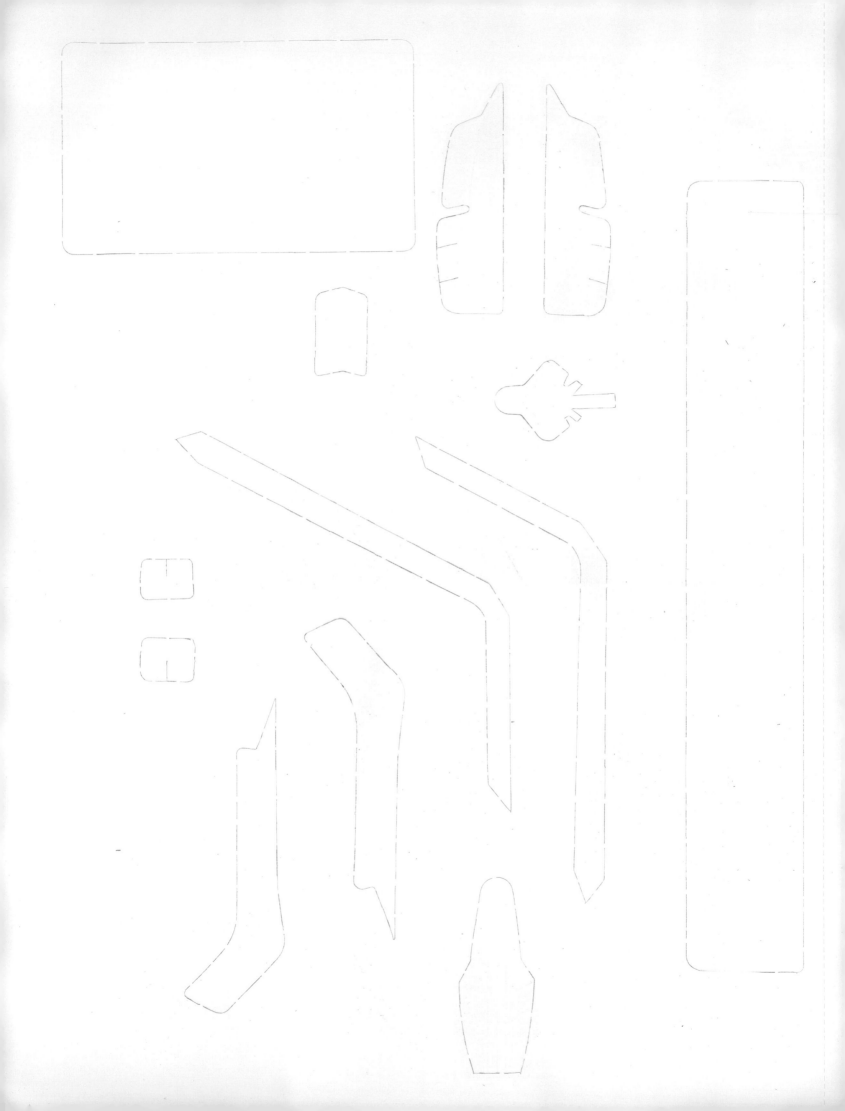

MAVRO

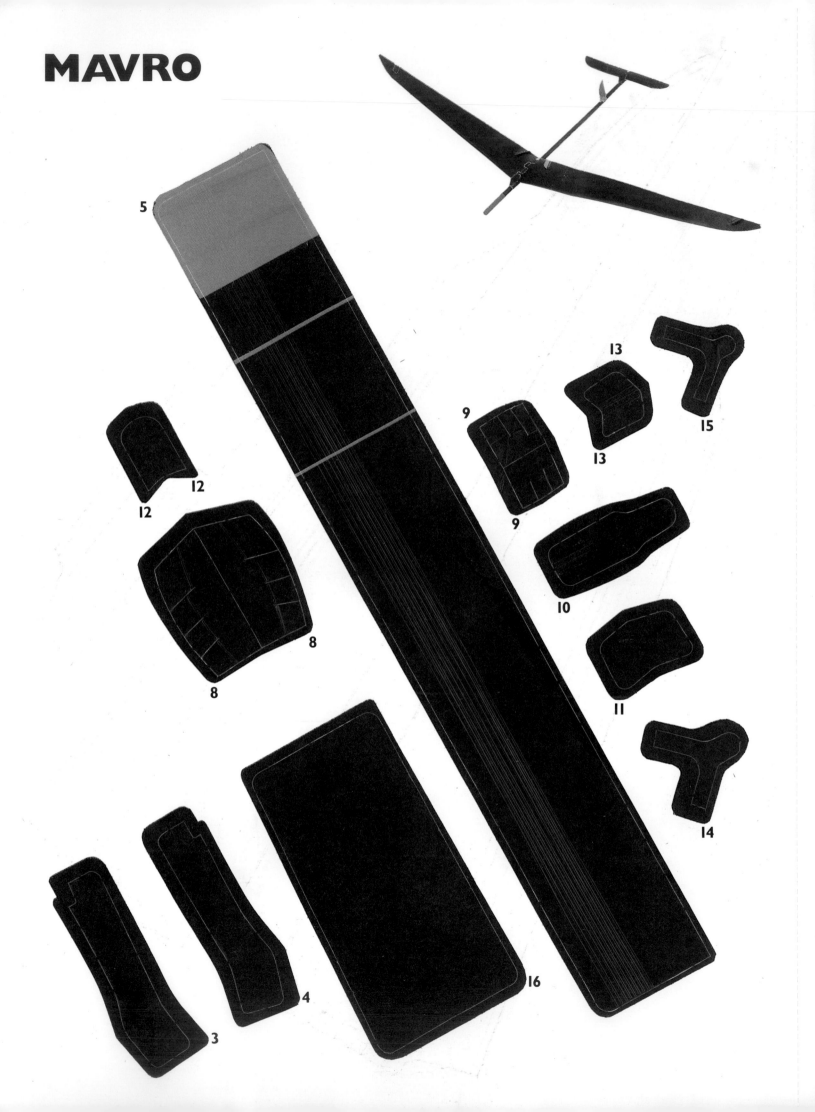

WHITE KNIGHT

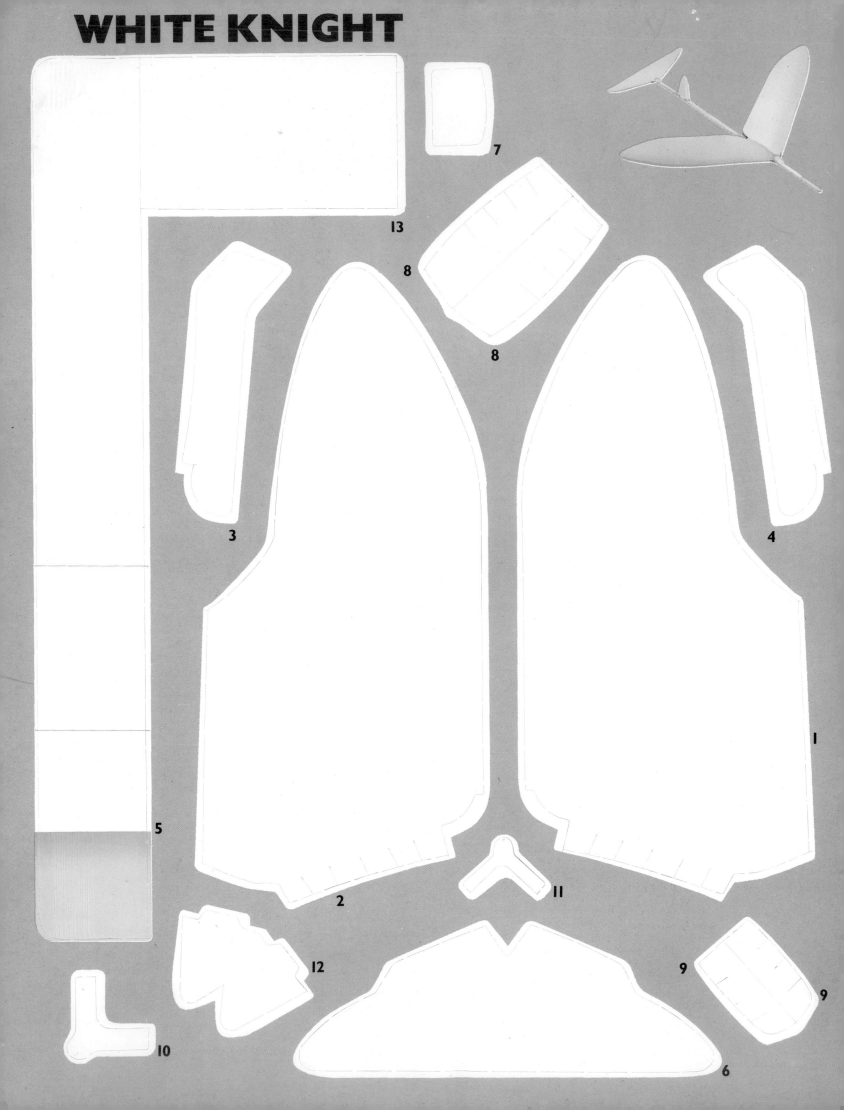